A Good Night's Sleep

By Allan Fowler

Consultants

Linda Cornwell, Learning Resource Consultant,
Indiana Department of Education

Fay Robinson, Child Development Specialist

Lynne Kepler, Educational Consultant

Children's Press®
A Division of Grolier Publishing
New York   London   Hong Kong   Sydney
Danbury, Connecticut

Project Editor: Downing Publishing Services
Designer: Herman Adler Design Group
Photo Researcher: Caroline Anderson

Library of Congress Cataloging-in-Publication Data

Fowler, Allan.
    A good night's sleep / by Allan Fowler.
      p. cm. – (Rookie read-about science)
    Includes index.
    Summary: Provides information about the need for sleep and effects
of its lack, sleepwalking, dreaming, animals that sleep and dream, nocturnal
animals, and hibernation.
    ISBN 0-516-20030-5 (lib. bdg.) — ISBN 0-516-26081-2 (pbk.)
    1. Sleep—Juvenile literature. [1. Sleep.] I. Title. II. Series
QP425.F67   1996
612.8'21—dc20   96-14013
                                                           CIP
                                                           AC

What's the one thing you
do more than anything else?
You sleep!

You spend far more
time sleeping than you
do playing or eating or
going to school.

You don't go to school every day. But you do sleep every night.

Here's what would happen if you didn't get enough sleep at night. You'd feel tired and yawn a lot . . .

you couldn't keep your
mind on what you were
doing . . . you'd start
making mistakes . . .

and you'd doze off
during the day.

You need plenty of sleep
to stay healthy, feel good,
and keep growing.

Most grownups sleep
about seven or eight
hours a night.

You probably sleep
a little more.

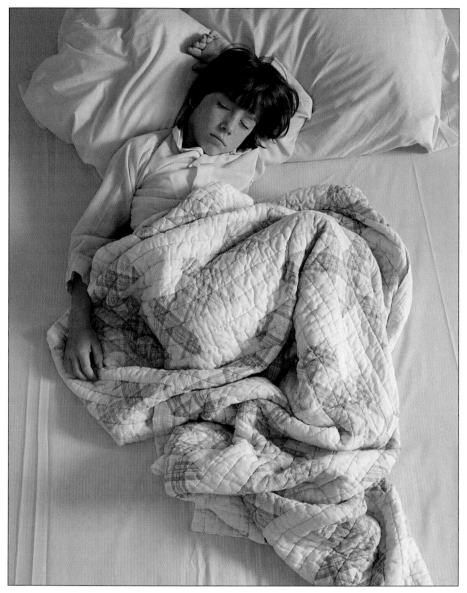

12

Your body moves around many times while you're asleep.

A few people get out of bed and walk around in their sleep.

After they wake up, they don't remember sleepwalking. Many people talk in their sleep — or snore.

When you sleep, you dream.

Everybody dreams every night. But we forget most of our dreams when we wake up.

We're only likely to remember a dream if we wake up during the dream or right after it.

15

Did you ever wake up in the middle of a dream . . .

and think the dream was something that was really happening?

Dreams can fool you that way, or sometimes scare you.

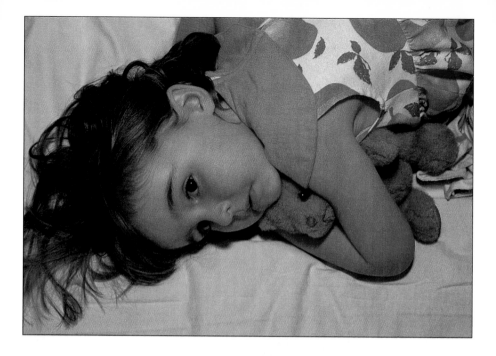

As soon as you wake up from a bad dream, just remember that a dream is like a story. It's not really happening.

Fortunately, most dreams are pleasant. They don't always make much sense, though you might get a good idea from a dream.

Do animals sleep?
Mammals and birds do.

Fish and insects don't seem to, although they do slow down and rest at times.

Cows can sleep standing up!

Scientists have learned that mammals dream.

What do you suppose a dog or a cat dreams about?

23

Certain animals, such as bats and owls, sleep during the day and are awake at night.

That's when they hunt
for food. They are called
nocturnal animals.

Chipmunks and some other animals hibernate.

That is, they sleep through the coldest part of the winter, when food would be hard to find.

The food that's already stored in their bodies as fat keeps them alive while they sleep.

Hibernating is fine
for chipmunks, but not
for people.

You wouldn't want to sleep
right through the winter
holidays, would you?

Words You Know

sleep

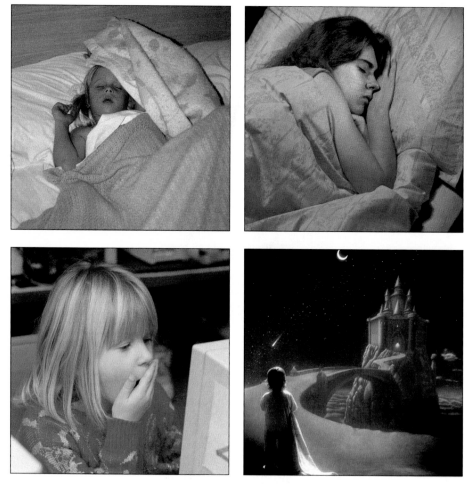

yawn   dream

nocturnal animals

owl

bat

hibernation

chipmunk

Index

About the Author

Allan Fowler is a free-lance writer with a background in advertising. Born in New York, he lives in Chicago now and enjoys traveling.

Photo Credits

©Comstock — cover, 5, 9

Valan Photos — ©Dr. A. Farquhar, 3, 29; ©Val & Alan Wilkinson, 19; ©John Mitchell, 21; ©J.A. Wilkinson, 23; ©Wayne Lankinen, 24, 31 (top left); ©Kennon Cooke, 26 (background)

Photo Researchers, Inc. — ©Rita Nannini, 4; ©Andrew M. Levine, 6, 30 (bottom left); ©J. Gerard Smith, 8; ©Sheila Terry/Science Photo Library, 10, 30 (top right); ©Richard Hutchings, 15; ©Merlin D. Tuttle, 25, 31 (top right); ©Leonard Lee Rue III, 26 (inset), 31 (bottom)

Tony Stone Images, Inc. — ©Don Bonsey, 16, 30 (bottom right); ©David J. Sams, 18

SuperStock International, Inc. — ©Vincent Hobbs, 7

Visuals Unlimited — ©John D. Cunningham, 11, 30 (top left); ©Tom Edwards, 20; ©Richard Thom, 29

Folio, Inc. — ©Pat Lanza Field, 12

COVER: Sleeping child